Ellen Wehle has taught poetry and creative writing, sold timeshares on the beach, and once edited at an ad agency—where she learned more about cruise-ship cabins than she ever wanted to know. She lives with her husband and two dogs in Chicago, where she does her best writing while hurtling underground on the L.

ELLEN WEHLE

The Ocean Liner's Wake

Shearsman Books
Exeter

First published in the United Kingdom in 2009 by
Shearsman Books Ltd
58 Velwell Road
Exeter EX4 4LD

www.shearsman.com

ISBN 978-1-84861-071-2
First Edition

Acknowledgements

*ACM, Blue Mesa Review, Christianity and Literature, Colorado State Review,
Crazyhorse, 88, Epoch, FIELD, The Grove Review, GSU Review, Gulf Coast,
The Iowa Review, Larcom Review, LUNA, New England Review, The New
Republic, Notre Dame Review, Oregon Review, Poetry International, Runes, Slate,
Southern Humanities Review, The Southern Review, Versal,
Washington Square, Web Conjunctions, West Branch, Westerly.*

'Face' received the Chicago Literary Award from *Another Chicago Magazine.*

'The Song of 10' was reprinted in *Poetry International*, appeared on *Poetry
Daily*, and was included in the anthology *Strange Attractors: Mathematical
Love Poems.*

Special thanks to The Poetry Center of Chicago, The Rehoboth Beach
Writers' Conference, and The Elizabeth George Foundation, without
whose generous support I could not have completed this book.

Cover image, 'Starry Night of Brazil', copyright © Babak Tafreshi, 2009.

Contents

For my husband,
who gave the possible life

Given Happiness Like Water

Who wouldn't be the reed basket, rain-hollowed stone?
Always borne aloft in other arms
God knows we are only half-human
That truth is a spiral staircase
Why should we grieve
Windrows of tasseled corn flowing past the road
Like the wake of an ocean liner
Astronomers track the star's signal backward to time's
Source, its cloud of dust and gas like the wake
Of an ocean liner, windrows of tasseled corn flowing
My darling why should we grieve
That truth is a spiral staircase
God knows we are only half-human
Always borne aloft in other arms
Who wouldn't be the reed basket, rain-hollowed stone?

I

The Song of 10

From the Romans' *decem* our decibels and decimal
system, O tenfold the sorrows of Israel, Decameron

tales told over ten days in December, solstice month
frozen in moondrifts of snow. Our fingers and toes.

Kingly ten-point stags ruling Europe's greenwoods,
for miners a measure in tons of coal or type of tallow

candle weighted ten per pound, the legion poor sewing
by its glow. What else is there to say? Higher than nine.

A number whose power is great to multiply, comprising
one and nil, wand and egg, spindle and heavenly wheel

of goddess Fate who turns time and tides; or what our
parents say summer evenings, hearing our voices dart

and flicker in neighboring yards before we dance from
them into darkness and the world ends, *I'll count to ten.*

Saturday Morning

Once when I was a child I ate a wand of the Hansens' forsythia.

Why? A frenzy of lust—March skies, forsythia blowing like spray off a fountain.

How I wrestled with that bush. Wood fresh and full of sap, I can't say it was easy.

Is it Piaget who speaks of differentiation, knowing you are *this* because you are not *that*?

Honey-scented it lay across my palm. It was not me.

A lifetime ago and still I taste that betrayal. Goddamn forsythia bitter as radishes, as cellar dirt. The Hansens staring from their breakfast table.

Yellow fire dripping off my tongue.

How to Get Struck by Lightning

Court destruction. Barometer plunging,
      keep tapping the glass. Anger the gods,

make absurd claims, *My works shall*
      live forever. Throw open windows, smash

the willow china. Know treetops shake
      in ecstatic fits. At sky's first electric tongue-

flick, transformation enters the story:
      Medusa-like your hair will lift, veins fizz.

Relax, it's normal. Calculate odds,
      place your stake—yourself—laughing

on the shingled rooftop, a steeple. Ignite.

Gravity

People don't jump off bridges because they want to die. Perched
on the swaying cables, we have never loved life more. Clinging,
hands gone dumb, the pigeon shit, the strata of molted feathers.
Exultation: two dark wings, a door.

⋆

When I was sixteen the Blue Route hung unfinished in the sky,
phantom sections of highway that would connect Philadelphia to
Allentown. No reason. We'd park and scale the cliff up to girders:
me, the boy who loved me. A single catwalk strung over the valley.
Edging out. Stars hot as spilled rocket fuel.

⋆

I look for it still. Body bowing out from the iron struts, gravity
a key dropped from my lap. Then . . . slowly . . . the letting go.
Right strut. Left. His hand between my shoulder blades; my life
locked in his fist. Far below, a rumble of wheels, the magnificat
of freight trucks passing.

Absolute Zero

Matter's lowest attainable point; electrons stop circling.

Four a.m. Awake again.

Tenth grade, that guy at the 63rd Street terminal. *Hey girl, wanna
    get high?* Voice dipping. *Wanna fuck?*

Zen concept of relation: energy transferred through the collision
    of individuals.

Of course I kept on walking.

We are given this weapon of ourselves: our napes, the small of our
    backs. *Yesss* rising from my solar plexus.

And the soul? A blackboard of equations.

Certain words, he once told me, *carry enough current to light up
    entire cities.*

Tonight's droning faucet.

Fuck . . . fuck . . . f . . .

Key Hidden In Case of Emergency

Secret forgotten I circumnavigate our house

★

Always the trellis, ornamental, refusing human weight

★

Train that bore me here long since gone

★

Moon keeps her counsel on whatever gleams, jewel-like,
        Cut to fit my palm

★

Abracadabra I say but the eyelid only flutters

★

First this latch, then that

Flute

Spendthrift my neighbor leaves all lights burning

*

Rain forces the ferns slowly down

*

After long sleep, how the nerves quiver: one note
    A knife ascending

*

Some arpeggio the neighbor's child keeps playing

*

Window, how will I bear it

*

Throbbing *oh, oh*, until she strikes true

Hymn

Scarab tethered to a nail, I circle the question

*

Have I wandered so far from myself

*

East, West, the compass-points glowing

*

Granite stela worn to sand

*

O Invisible, trailing your wake of broken starlight

*

Span between us *ad infinitum* halved

Soul

She has left the city of bones

Would rather inhabit
Clock-hollows

Blows out lit pilots
Say we remember the hurtling

Forward every pulsebeat
A path through thorns

If only we could name that pinhole
Inside us, asterisk she

Enters, exits, depth
Charge lighting the waters

She moves ever

One breath beyond us
Elevator chime sounding night's

Coal chute, our voices
Telegraph-clicks, whiteout

Descending she leaves *body*
A bank-vault

Laid bare without
Her how else to explain these hours

Struggling to rise beneath
My own weight

Houdini Escapes

Black lacquer boxes
Slow-fuse cannons
Crates nailed tight

Not even a scratch
Just keeps returning
In padlocks in iron

Cuffs dragging his
Secret behind him
That steamer trunk

Loaded with bricks
Flung in East River
Jack-in-the-pulpit

He pops from a milk
Jug a humongous
Milk jug flanked

By two English
Bobbies such a calm
Stare straitjacketed

Hung by the heels
Over Broadway
Can't you see yet

Where we're headed
Chained to a great
Locomotive he says

To his wife *Open*
Your mouth he says
On his deathbed

He says *With a kiss*
I'll pass my key
From the black box

Maw of the cannon

Poem Ending with a Line from the Pharaohs

Still, Newton got it wrong.
Pebbles flung off bridges
Do not sink but, rather,

Marry water. It's the way
Icons operate: the more
Deeply you hold a saint's

Eye the deeper she takes
You in, pupil a nebula.
How long at this threshold,

Child, have you lingered.
Considering catwalks over
Urban streets are girdled

In mesh-guard to curtail
Not falling but leaping,
You can be excused that

Desire to dance (first, only
Pennies) off your office's
Six-inch rock-dove ledge,

Oceans of asphalt calling.
In the same way opposing
Poles on any horseshoe

Magnet acquire proximity
By means of a hard bend,
Let's tell the Milky Way

Yes, let's race to meet the
Tide tomorrow, *Weigh my
Heart against a feather.*

Five Variations on a Theme

I
Occasionally he talked about bombing the Ruhr Valley.
Dams shaken apart by shock waves.
Altitude so low he could see frantic cars as they raced the roar.
  Headlights briefly gleaming underwater.

II
Centuries later submersibles find proof of the forty days.
Beneath the Black Sea: sawn lumber, amphorae intact with wine,
  heaps of riprap.
Like a temple whose gods have gone, the sunken coastline.

III
My uncle lived through the flood. At the end it was all he'd say,
  as a boy he boated down Main Street.
Coming home we'd slow the car.
High above the toolworks that tidemark stenciling the brick.

IV
In case of drowning, stop struggling; open your mouth.
In Cornwall it's understood.
No fisherman will float you an oar, but watch at a distance while
  the river takes a new spouse.

V

If the universe can be a Word, it can be erased. Barefoot on
    deck Noah prays to thunderheads.

Five Forms Prayer Takes

Door ajar to invite
Forces moving
Fog-like among us
To enact our designs

★

Heart in a winepress
Hoarse down-calling
Lords, gods, angels,
Preserve me from evil
Plots and disease

★

At the farthest shore
Of our wandering
Self a gurgle in the walls
Bathwater's long echo

★

Even as a Golden
Ratio the nautilus
Spirals ever inward
Chambering quiet

★

Droplet suspended
Question left
Pearled on the lip
Of a milk glass

Call

When Stalin's bombs
Started raining on Berlin
All the telephones rang
At once, concussive
Blasts vibrating bedrock

★

Hello? Let this take you
To the next place

★

Joint-wrack, pulse-tide,
Syncopated lumen of nerves,
I don't believe I am alone
In making an enemy
Of my own body

★

Here I have been
Knocking, Rumi says,
From the inside

★

Votress of the spinning
Dust motes, of jade-green
Tea just poured . . . yes,
I understand long illness,
Pain as chanticleer

★

Tooth-edge, moon-
Shard, how to
Hover short of waking

★

Whatever hurries toward me
Trembling the ground
Light's catenary arc, bulbs
Strung along the subway tunnel

★

Merely answer your door

★

Inexplicable tonight,
The dog—how she keeps
Crying, foxy ears
Pricked forward, eyes
Fixed on mine

Consciousness

Sack of rocks we drag.
Telescope dish turning.

Engine-hum in back
Alleys where all night

Trucks idle their load,
Whomever the Devil

Would destroy . . . how
Does that saying go?

Can we not silence
It even half an hour:

Slip off our headset,
Forget the last ship's

Tinny SOS, break out
Champagne and party.

Palace of a thousand
Lamps left burning

Far below the waves.
. . . *he first makes wise.*

There is a Country Called the Past
Which Will Not Release Me

Night pins me to the edge of a pool, virgin, afraid to get high
    or jump in.

Florida, a transom of stars. Sabal palm trees' bony rattle.

All of us had locked up the bar, shed our aprons—that pool
    lapis blue as the arc of his eye.

Afraid to breathe. Afraid to plunge in.

Ilium

With what great wisdom the world forbids our pleasures to last

                           Joy chooses us and darts away

For what wouldn't we give a lover

                    Like the dragonfly that lit on the end of my oar

To defer that moment and linger

                                   Gilded herald

Perpetually

                    Balanced between sky and water

In the pelvic cradle

                               I watched him tremble

Bones speaking to bones

And the kingdom inside me went still

We say let the legion stars extinguish

                        Let me dwell here forever

And as one trace the arc of

                        His beauty almost unbearable

Hipbones the ilium

                        Wings rising and falling in place

Which like the walls of Troy

                        But we know where this moment's headed

Enclosing what is most valuable

                        Travel the sole purpose of any particle-wave

Lead us into the sacred city

In the end I must cross the lake

II

Michaelmas

Now that wild five-pointed leaves
Glut Sagamore's gutters
Furnace men have come and gone
Lowering stair by stair their promise of heat
Frost crystals fracture
And strangers remark *such milky skin*
Skein of blue veins visible
Now that misgiving gathers power
True North erased from the map of my palm
Wind tutors the ivy
Eaves *keep yourself a secret*
Our house hunkers down around us
Now that we know happiness
Means few notes actually sung on key
Oddments of isinglass shiny and easily broken
Daylight slips from us orphans
In the interval between
Sin and its wages our foreheads pulse
Against the world
Eight glazed panes hang fire

Custody

Flathead screws
Brass lock laid sideways
My husband planes and mutters
As if we could keep
Out that arctic history
Draft prying at the jambs
We know so much
Heads south so quickly
Damage done I make dinner
Her kids silent at the kitchen table
Signal lamps flicker
Alone pacing the shore
Merchant tankers scrawl the water
Throw me a line
Harms I have no hand to mend
Lambs-wool unravels
Winthrop's seawall one long
Crumble the republic of this family
Whatever no one's saying
Under my roof now

We Say the Wind

Hotel balcony. Night city
Jewel-cut, light-decked
Trees. Ornamental
Pond a looking-glass struck once,
Undulant. What to name
Wind's talent for continuously
Leaving? Monks raking
Gravel the concentric circles
Rippling, mariners
Dead-reckoning speed and course
By current . . . truly awesome
Is the mystery of breath,
Soul's bond to body so tirelessly
Broken. Snow considers
Falling, park-lights halo, fog
Crystals forming at our
Lips we bow like
Reeds, in Latin *exit*—he goes.

Face

Mega moisture cream releases worn out
cells to reveal youthful texture and tone

Salvation as almond paste or attar of rose
Consider all lost the empire
Undone to rubbled pillar and vine
Consider Roman martyrs
Ablaze *I thought I knew what I chose*
Would change me Time leaning
Over human coals to light
His torch consider
It's too late to call off the party
Lifeboats thrown topside as floe ice
Luminesces signal rockets
Scatter *Baby this ship's going under*
Those blithe summers sprawled
Across the flower state's powder-sugar
Sands no one wants to live
Forever so why twitch
In pain passing every plate-glass window
Beads of rain suspended sea
Fog to sea you wake up one morning
Wolf whistles absent in the streets

Loft

Because I'd wandered too far
From myself the sea
Sent me an ache
My right hip a kiln
Aglow all winter
Water pipes moaned cello
Notes downed wires
Sparked on asphalt that joint
Radiant in foul weather
Because gulls never stop circling
Larger questions of worth
Dash onto rocks
Maiden oysters in bracelets
Of seaweed the sacrum
Cradle-bone our lives just keep
Grinding must I fashion
Myself again from a great
Height white days
Adrift in bed Persian
Ivy braced the opposite building

Fortieth Birthday as Bosch's
Death and the Miser

But first
One last grand party
Spilled light through a dormer window
Vellum sealed with scarlet wax
I kept my other life closeby
High in the rafters no one watching
How on earth we get through our days
Woodsmoke and hatchmarks
Hours dragged under
Riptide in that upstairs bedroom our host's
Trapdoor snapped wide we shot
Straight down lips forming
Cartoon O's . . . Transmigration . . . simply
Snow geese scribing the eastern sky if I could
Gloss the message meant for me
Dancer's footwork a gilded
Glancing blow someone
Calling *a candle a candle* in our darkness
Unable to see we had long left
The tunnel behind us

Calamity

Our sun rose and they were here
Coal-scatter   dragon's spine   boulders
Washed up at our door
Extending the shore far out to sea
In strips the paint peeled while the painter slept
For no further reason
Nobody could stand the thirteenth fairy at the feast
Lobbing her curses apple-high
Let's leave it unsaid
Household poisons perform swiftly
Gas pedal jammed at sixty   still we wondered
What that keening meant
Each time smoke alarms wobbled
And me half-asleep unplugging the phone
Astronauts orbiting Earth
Claim roofless space has an odor
Acrid as burnt metal   all those unheeded prayers
Give us a sign flying like photons
Was this the nail
For lack of which our kingdom would be lost

To Destruction

Sea-salt that blanches the beach stairs
Absinthe over crushed ice
O wrecking ball, O poison bud
Marking our exit from Eden
O stretch of track behind my street
Where high school boys outran the train
O engineer who stomped the brake three miles
Reason a well-worn Bible always
Falls open at Revelations
If not loveliness, if not suffering
Who wouldn't welcome Armageddon
As long as we could watch it? O flickering
Bracelet of campfires as Vikings circled Paris
Seven trumpets sounding
Astronauts hurtling earthwards
Columbia's insulation tiles snowflakes in a furnace
O nearly nothing that was left
O teeth, O teeth, embedded in his grille

To the Boys Skateboarding on Boston Common

Don't prate to us of love
As the promissory
Kingdom when we are
Stones thrown through windows,
Barbed arrows V'd in flight,
Green hunger risen from grassblades,
Flat on our backs all summer.
One Cessna, one thought
Circling; heat-hazed the city's distant
Generators hum. We say no
Harm intended, glass
Shivers to be
Broken. Who cares if light
Waves made us? Atriums, our bodies
Cannot speak, remember
Nothing.

To the Bride Posing for Photos
in Millennium Park

Why is the ravishing moment
Not sonata but that lull
After, as violins
Scrape and cough?
Delight's undernote of jangle.
Rose of Sharon tossing
Scent in fistfuls, you pass, love
Loud as a door-slam.
Now let us sing in praise
Of pain to come *Western wind*
When wilt thou blow, that
Little twitch we
Make at brink of sleep,
Far from shore, far
From the linkboys' torches.
Love an iceberg. Gored-out hull.
Those women, shawled,
Bathrobed, who
Though lifeboats lowered
Would not leave their husbands.

Leave Your Doors Wide Open

Increasingly as the natural world
Withdrew, our firmament
Filled with numbers. *Fulgura frango,*
Sang the bells, *I break*
Lightning. Rattling my bone china.
Once the split oak gathered
Up rooks and fell quiet, *let it be done.*
Wary, then, I caught myself
In a series of small lies.
Amplified by rain, footsteps crossing
Toward me. Clouds percussed
As if to promise anything
Could still happen even at this late
Date: stopped dead
On the staircase landing,
Arms anchored with laundry.
As dairymen candle an egg, here too
The white-hot judgment,
Razzle of light— In case thunder
Should enter your
House, hungry for egress.

Collective History Verging on My Sleep

Heifer dark of eye
Abandoned at the altar steps
Anguished and lowing
If there were only some governing order
If DNA would codify our nature
Braiding helixes the way
Equal signs started
Life as a glyph for water
Synchronous scullers glide their oars
In the beginning every outcast
Star crowned in dust
Waltzing round the black hole's rim
Body's telegraph frantically
Tapping my life sheet
Lightning that strikes not-quite-me
Girl as faraway shore
Thus the Garden before pruning
Risen by flood of evening whoever comes
To whet my shears
Who turns the grinding-stone

III

Snow Falling All Morning, I Read the Egyptian "Negative Confession"

In this house of windows watching

> *Lord in my time on earth*

Naked to the world

> *I did no evil*

As saplings like white deer

> *Did not steal milk from the mouth of a child*

Scrape past bent low

> *Alter the weights of the balance*

By all means remind me again

> *Blow out your flame*

How suffering is beauty

> *Blazing in the temple against darkness*

Even the birches graced unto death

> *Give anyone cause to weep*

Keep trembling 'yes'

I am pure, pure, pure

While I remain a pane of glass

Seat me at your right hand

In Key West the Kids Want to Tour Ripley's Museum

First, we are flesh.

★

Candlefish carrying our wicks
inside us, we spend
ourselves head and foot, prodigally.

★

What the kids like to see: loose eyeballs,
Sioux braves hanging by fishhooks
from the ceiling.

★

Up close the Iron Maiden smiles.
Gown agape, her breasts
naked as doves, as if to say *Come,*
pain is your mother.

★

Entrance, exit.

★

Explain the mystery yourself. Why saintliness
so compels us, we see it and reach
for the knife.

★

I have caused suffering.
Have stood peeling an orange and watched.

*

I saw the iron enter his soul. Idiom for
he suffers, meaning tools of injury
tend to be iron-forged.

*

Silhouetted against snowfall
in that open doorway,
really, I knew what he was asking.

*

And Key West? Hibiscus trailing soft
gasps down a sun-washed
wall, parrots—of course—in droves.

Chronic

Meaning *time*. Pity the spine its staircase of rickety scaffolding.
Tendons strung like piano wire, the faintest tap of the hammer:

we shiver with pain. Pouring foundations for a mall, the bog
chieftain is unearthed with his prehistoric cure, each vertebra

ringed in blue-ash tattoo. *Are you conscious of a soul separate
from the body, or do you see your body as yourself.* Who drags

us forward over the wheel of days? Corpus, spiritus, as married
as the emperor to Rome. A boy I knew once sliced his forearm

on a rock, his mother flat-out screaming to see perforated skin,
afraid his soul leaked out. Cellar windows left open all summer.

Two digging thumbs settle any question of my existence, nailed
to a compass-point I am here O zigzag bones, O radiant star of

pain as Jim the masseur natters about sculpture, "The Prisoners"
sunk in marble struggling to throw free a falcate arm, a throat,

take this cup away from me, body's long apprenticeship to ruin.
Meanwhile soul doesn't give a damn. Crowned, robed in purple,

fiddling as Rome burns down to a sea-coal, handful of hot cinder.

Sunday Mass

Because my stepdaughter ran with a rough crowd, every
week we wrestled her to church like sailors unknot rope

to loose fair winds, the priest and his white stole invoking
that divine light which longs to be brought to earth in us

as my mind wandered away to last year's crop of glorious
failures (how I called the in-laws drunks, hid from howls

behind my open book) which I've been told comprise real
life, scored-out pages littering carpets in abandoned rooms

the only music Heaven hears though our concertos thunder
on. My intention to *simply be love*: that ballerina who took

a dive in her fairyland tiara and slippers. Four rows back
from the orchestra we couldn't help but see her wide-open

surprise as thirty dancers swayed together like candelabra
in a draft, like cattails by a lake and she flew up, sat down

hard, and the future with its snowy woods dropped into her.

Pyromancy

Because I have mistaken my
life: sparks tend to fly under attic eaves.
Free oxygen ignites.

Because I would rather bear
buckets of water. Because our daughter
burns so beautifully

her adolescence into ashes.
Flambeau, whichever way she flows
she draws all eyes.

Because of a certain sameness
to disaster. Newborn we too began,
a handful of tinder.

Although our ladders clang
along her roof. Muttering, asleep, she
speaks arson's tongue.

Girl gone up like a match
struck, all December scrying hearthfire
we glimpse bowers.

The Book of Hours: January

The Limbourg brothers, 1412–1416

Retired, my father repairs rare books. More empty days, he says,
    than he can fill.

I turn the page. Drowsy afternoon, my half-drunk tea steaming.

Yes, these are the beautiful hours.

Robed in ermine, the duke feasts. Courtiers stretch their hands
    to the flames as a chamberlain bids them, Come in,
    come in!

Far away, my father plies his craft. Threads glue along the spines.

While outside the ocean of snow deepens.

Only now, late, do I understand his love: bent over a table, lamp
    burning on and on.

Time . . . a figure-eight of geese in the falling sky.

The Fall of the Rebel Angels

The Limbourg brothers, 1412–1416

Another record of disaster. God blazing like a bonfire as rows
    of startled angels tumble from their chairs.

A girl's voice at the library: "I knew I could hurt him, so I did."

Centuries ago the artist shivers in a draft.

"Then he was gone."

Steadily dips his brush, crushes petals in a mortar.

Bone-cold wind beneath the door.

Angels hurtle down. Faces frozen in dismay, palms on fire.
    Unknowable, he thinks, the mystery.

Yes, alright: I was the girl.

Why blithely we hazard what we love.

Building the Cathedrals

If a ladder takes
A man's life in

That a tumble
Back to earth

Cracks open his
Head, by Saxon

Law the culprit
Must burn, its

Life recompense.

★

Ceiling star-hung.
When I promise

You the heavens
Close at hand,

Ascend me, love,
With great care.

Grain-deep my
Oldest fear: I

Crown the pyre.

Gargoyle, Sainte Mère Église

Company F was called for a briefing . . . they would be dropped,
under cover of night, in the fields outside of town.

As if created for no other
        End but this smoke-filled Boschian
           Sky of flailing legs

Openmouthed men
        (Free-falling silk parachute
           Blossoms)

Caroming against the stone
        Church's belfry; as if our life was
           Not one long

Daisy chain of hazard
        Missed moments and chances to
           Fail; had the Allied

Pilot flying through heavy
        Cloud not mistaken the mapped drop
           Zone or Hairon's

Barn not burned quite so
        Brightly like a beacon on invasion
           Night . . . but they

Did, they did, Private Russell
    Skittering down the roof-tiles unable
    To break his

Fall sees cobblestone below
    Germans gawking at these God-given
    Targets gutter–

Edge precipice feels himself
    Go before one mighty yank behind
    Him and he's

Snag, thump. Saved.

The Hanging of Judas in Reverse Order

For years I hovered at my own threshold.

An ivy-twined trunk.

Here in the garden, shade's column of cold air. High C hit at
    Perfect pitch.

Love a plumb-line drop onto railroad tracks.

A waiting we never come back from.

And then silence. Quarry bottom. Fronds swaying silt.

This is the past, you say, lying deep as the moon's wake after
    Lit cities roar by.

I know, I know.

If Not the Bliss We Were Promised

If stars sing in our blood of trace metals

If atomic clocks rely on excitation

Sap rising up sugar maples

How many winters of white sleep

I awaited that arrival

If our fingertips house a hundred nerves

Each lit with alchemical fire

Name my race dust name me void's daughter

If half-dead I just kept choosing

Light frozen to a solid

What else could it be this brilliant

Pane the fly is drawn to

Fragment of a Tomb Wall

Limestone, Egypt, 2700 BC

Because it remains a feast
        Unfinished. What's brought

Me here again: slaughtered
        Beasts crowned in flowers,

A Last Judgment of feathers,
        Loaves piled high . . . princeling

And his kohl-eyed wife dead
        Center, seated. Four maidens

Fan the congregation, each
        Butcher grappling a foreleg

Oxen bawl on their backs,
        Nose to earth. Number me

Among you. Because no one
        Here retains their requisite

Parts: I, too, who've passed
        Certain days below, embark

By knife. Or because veiled,
   Hidden in the reeds along

Stone's margin a single fish
   In motion, spark flying up . . .

Sharps

As for adoration's

Tools, a corner turned I can no longer

Bear the sight of them

Fruit knives, iris scissors

Needles winking with one eye

Implements of entry

Ushering the world—what's outside—

In keeping with the butcher's

Block that keens before

Each blow I face each morning: gull-cry

Sea stone calm

Vapor rising off Salem Harbor, that same

Old problem rapture poses

If as they say the severed

Worm forgives the plough, how shall we

Understand ourselves—soft

Open hearts-as-mouths, devourers

Of the dark—a longing most

Alive cut to pieces

IV

The Dream of the Hive

Gray rains at first a rumor
Voice of the beloved
Calling us to sleep

Little pharaoh with my days
Laid beside me

Honeysuckle and lilac

Grains of gold-dust
Up to the rafters
Cells full of provender

*

Compel us to hum

In sure and certain faith
Sun resurrect me
Whatever harms I may

Commit still I remember
Where we come
From . . . where we go . . .

Hollow oak heart

Flying buttresses of wax
Word cracking across
Time and space

★

And wake into that other
Kingdom: Clover
By orders of magnitude

Honey of such
Vintage sweet spit
Tufts of fur

Flowering pear . . .